Broken to be Healed

Broken to be Healed

"The Lord hath appeared of old unto me, saying, Yea, I have loved thee with an everlasting love: therefore with loving kindness have I drawn thee." (Jeremiah 31:3 KJV) (1)

Yvonne M. Nelson

XULON PRESS ELITE

Xulon Press Elite
2301 Lucien Way #415
Maitland, FL 32751
407.339.4217
www.xulonpress.com

© 2021 by Yvonne M. Nelson

All rights reserved solely by the author. The author guarantees all contents are original and do not infringe upon the legal rights of any other person or work. No part of this book may be reproduced in any form without the permission of the author. The views expressed in this book are not necessarily those of the publisher.

Due to the changing nature of the Internet, if there are any web addresses, links, or URLs included in this manuscript, these may have been altered and may no longer be accessible. The views and opinions shared in this book belong solely to the author and do not necessarily reflect those of the publisher. The publisher therefore disclaims responsibility for the views or opinions expressed within the work.

Unless otherwise indicated, Scripture quotations taken from the King James Version (KJV)–public domain.

Printed in the United States of America.

Paperback ISBN-13: 978-1-6628-1486-0
eBook ISBN-13: 978-1-6628-1487-7

Dedication

To my children Tiffany Marie Murry
and Timothy Lee Murry 11

Thank you both for giving me a reason to grow and heal towards my wholeness. As you both travel through your own passage of brokenness, may you find yourselves in the Grace of God for your wholeness and restoration. May the love of God massage both your hearts and resuscitate your life in the palm of His hands.

Table of Contents

Chapter 1
Perception 1

Chapter 2
Saturated by His Love 7

Chapter 3
Surrender 15

Chapter 4
Paradigm Shift 21

Chapter 5
Silence 29

Chapter 6
Dark Season 35

Chapter 7
The Spirit of Oppression 43

Chapter 8
Deliverance 53

Chapter 9
God's Mercies 65

Chapter 10
Grace 79

Conclusion
Work in Progress 85

Forwarded

BY JOYCE M. BECKFORD

Having read Yvonne M. Nelson's book, "Broken to Be Healed," I found myself looking back in perspective at my own life. This book reminds me of God's faithfulness and grace in the life of all his children.

In all of us there is or will be brokenness; but God who is our ultimate healer takes us through a journey and brings us to total healing.

This book is a must read. It will equip you with the tools that you need for healing and spiritual growth. Within each page you will find the true meaning of someone, Yvonne M. Nelson, who was broken and now restored. She is still a work in progress as we all are in the Potter's hands.

She wrote this book, not from second hand experience, but she has lived through every page in this book. Yvonne is a very successful nurse. She brings spiritual and physical healing to her patients because God has equipped her through suffering and a yielding heart to use what was meant for evil for the good of others. I guarantee as you read this book, you will be passing this title around 'Broken to Be Healed" to all of your family members and friends.

Need healing? I highly recommend that you read this book. I did and it has been a delight.

Acknowledgement

Bishop Christopher-Don, thank you for the words of wisdom that you shared and for refocusing me when; rage could have easily over-powered me, suicide could have taken me, and hopelessness could have captured me. Thank you for your patient and listening ears as I cried, ranted and raged through my emotions and feelings of hopelessness. You kept my light burning when hope was dim. My protective instinct from my experiences, so vivid through the eyes of my son and daughter, awakened the emotional pain in my soul. I appreciate your time and prayers. I feel a final release because the bondages are broken for me, and eventually will be for both of my children to gain the victory over the giants in their lives. I am determined to expose the enemy with honesty and integrity with the grace of God. I dedicate my life to guiding my children on the road to their restoration, repentance and recommitment to their spiritual, emotional and physical well-being. With your support, guidance and prayers, I know that victory will prevail. Thank you again for honestly speaking the truth regardless of how it could have affected my spirit/mind.

It is in our struggles we find our inner strength and learn our righteous place in His presence. The road ahead may appear gloomy and difficult; but one thing we know for sure — His presence will prevail. If only we would extend our inner core to maximize His spirit within us and truly indulge His presence, we would escape the hurt that lingers. It is my belief that if we sustain this experience, we would enjoy God's true love, joy and peace within our lives. How great an accomplishment that would be. Wow, just to imagine such a state of being gives me chills.

Introduction

As I reflect upon my life over the years, I see the demonstration of God's grace. I have often read the poem "Footprints in the Sand" and I can truly understand God's explanation of the single foot print representing him carrying us through difficult times. The spiritual vision of my life is like being in a coma with few memories. There is a clear picture of how I exist daily and function in survival mode. My memories are vague as if it was a protective shield God provided to protect my brain cells. *"and behold, I am with thee, and will keep thee in all places whither thou goest, and will bring thee again into this land; for I will not leave thee, until I have done that which I have spoken to thee of" (Gen. 28:15 KJV).*

I am now able to see how my career has excelled both professionally and financially. I was in total emotional despair prior to the uprooted turmoil of my life. I compartmentalized each of my fears, worries, emotions and problems and built a wall that kept me from knowing my inner being and pushed away love. I could never believe anyone could really love me. My misguided perceptions propelled me into mixed emotions and confusion that alienated me from my family, healthy relationships and life experiences. I coped by becoming a perfectionist. Yet, I found myself lonely and unfilled, as I could never perfect my life.

Misconception, by definition in Webster's dictionary, is a view that is incorrect because it is based on faulty thinking and misunderstanding.(2) Perception by definition, is the ability to see, hear or become aware of something through the senses.(2) These two words are powerful in human development as life experiences are formed through our thoughts and feelings. So, from birth, our mind deciphers external stimulus as good or bad. These life experiences could be received in a positive or negative way which can be the beginning of life's journey into our development.

Thank God for my children. They allowed me to shower them with all the love within me, as I felt safe with their love for me. Through their eyes I saw the reflection of myself and began to heal. Through my healing and broken journey, I recognized they too were damaged from an unhealthy environment created in my marriage and childhood. My scars from a fragmented childhood were only magnified in a marriage filled with toxic words, actions and rejections. Unaware that no matter how I pretended and covered the toxic tracks, the undercurrent emotions leaked towards my children spirit, emotions and physical well-being. Thus, it led them to the well of brokenness, sadness and confusion about their destiny. What a disaster to understand and yet be totally unable to remove or repair the damage which was imprinted on their minds and emotions. I now live with the pain they experienced. I totally understand each intricate piece and feel hopeless to change the course they now travel. Having come to realize this devastating blue-print of my entire life, I surrender my flesh to the will of God with complete repentance and submission. I have begun a journey of healing.

Chapter 1

Perception

Our vision of a family is often not expressed and communicated effectively. It is rather understood silently. Each individual perception often portrays misguided beliefs. These beliefs often lead families to foster insecure relationships, and a lack of purpose or participation in the family vision. Many are left with pain, rejection, and low self-esteem from such misunderstandings. This bitterness could be avoided. Effective communication is the simple solution to clarify perceptions, rather than clinging to misguided believes. However, the ultimate decision lies within each of us, and the choices we make will come with consequences we must learn to accept.

Life may have tried us with crisis (in various shapes and forms); but that does not mean we have to settle for status-quo. We should never allow circumstance to dictate our attitude, personality or behavior. If we allow the crisis to run its course, while we focus on the positive, we would slay our giants and walk into the plan of God. Focusing on the positive would help to mitigate pain, rejection, low self-esteem, etc. Painful emotions often over-power our spiritual being and push us into the storms of life. We fulfill the plan of the enemy when we view only the negative. Whereas we can embrace the blessings of peace, joy and all the promises God designed especially for each of us. *"But ye are chosen generation, a royal priesthood, a holy nation, a peculiar people; that ye should shew forth the praises of him who hath call you out of darkness into his marvelous light"* (1 Pet. 2:9 KJV).

Often times, we have expectations or desires for our loved ones that they cannot accept or meet. In these moments, we have to accept their choice and not force our will upon them. We spend our lives from generation to generation disagreeing with family members' choices. As a result, a wedge is formed between relationships and family unity. This leave those that are hurt and lost alone on a painful journey. If we could communicate the family's vision effectively and enforced it, family bonds would be stronger. This would allow everyone to embrace appropriate choices that ultimately keep us connected to the family legacy.

Families are created by God to stand in unity, working together whether good, bad or indifferent. However, when we allow the enemy to bring strife between family members, we have opened the door to the greatest destruction. The spirit of strife breaks unity, harmony, peace, joy, grace and love; and everyone in some form or shape becomes broken. This brokenness is the beginning of our life's destruction. It moves toward pain, unforgivable grudges, hatefulness, bitterness etc... All these behaviors go against the fruit of the Spirit. ***"But the fruit of the spirit is love, joy, peace, long suffering, gentleness, goodness, faith, Meekness, temperance: against such there is no law" (Gal. 5:22-23 KJV)***.

It is important to understand that the choices we make throughout our journey are never casual, but critical with destiny within them. These choices often leave us disconnected from our love ones, family and friends who have some form of a positive impact upon our lives. I have had the privilege (through the eyes of others and my own journey) to experience how children perceive parental love, sibling rivalry or strife between other family members differently. Those perceptions become ingrained within us. We believe the stories through our eyes and we hold on to the disappointments and pain tightly within our souls. Out of the abundance of these, we develop defensive feelings which later become toxic and fester into hate.

We continue to interact as a family; but throughout the years, the wounds mount and lead to toxic feelings. As a result, our support system disintegrates as the division grows between the individual and the family. Thus begins the toxic journey that separates us. Our cultivated feelings develop and over-shadow our spirit, moral, ethical and personal space. *"The thief cometh not, but for to steal, and to kill, and to destroy: I am come that they might have life, and that they might have it more abundantly" (John 10:10 KJV).*

Joy decreases as we begin to feel pain, resentment, pride, low self-esteem, bitterness, etc. At that point, life becomes a journey of poor choices, bumps and bruises. Isolation become our greatest friend and protector which eventually leave us in a lonely place and with an empty soul. That great monster "strife" is now out of our control and brings separation and loneliness. Through strife we give the enemy great control of our mind, soul and emotions. The enemy's ultimate plan is to isolate us so that his voice captures our mind and thoughts drawing us into darkness. *"Be sober, be vigilant; because your adversary the devil, as a roaring lion, walketh about, seeking whom he may devour:" (1 Pet. 5:8 KJV).*

Toxic poison and vulgarity changes our personalities by forming us into someone we no longer recognize. We detour from who God had created us to be. Pain encountered by our deformed perceptions (created throughout our life experiences) has now dissected and reshaped our thought process. These thought processes that have devolved create within us something unacceptable. We become defensive in our relationships because we are convinced that everyone is waiting to consumed and demolish us. If the truth be told, no one has ever woken up with thoughts of us as they too are dealing with their own giants.

We spend years intertwining these toxic emotions and whirlwind dramas until our belief in them pushes us to solitary life. We build a wall so thick (similar to the Alcatraz island) to protect us when instead it has place us in our own prison. It places us away from the truth within ourselves and our true form of unique beauty created by God. We abort our blessings, relationships, peace, joy, love and spiritual growth. The saddest outcome is we pass toxic vulgarity to our children who continue to pass it to the next generation, etc. We also bring it along to every relationship we encounter in life.

Often times, failure in our children, self, relationships and family can cause us to lose control of our inner being and self. Death and sickness brings mixed emotions to every individual. I believe they are tools that allow everyone to take inventory of their lives. They provide each of us an opportunity to face our giants of regret, loneliness and guilt. Yet some leave this life still immersed in toxic feelings; some face their giants and transform their lives; and some remain numb in the prison they have created for themselves.

Trials and tribulations provide a season for one to pursue and seek opportunities to recover and refocus. Pain and emotional trauma become a flash-back through our mind during conversations or interactions with people in similar circumstances. So, we have to look within ourselves and own the pain and misguided perceptions. We have to forgive ourselves and others. If we seek God's forgiveness, how can we not forgive our brothers and sisters whom we perceived have wronged us? The importance of forgiveness is understanding our own faults and actions and release our offenders. The condemnation and judgement of others is clearly described in ***Mathew 7:3 "And why beholdest thou the mote that is in thy brother's eye, but considerest not the beam that is in thine own eye?" (KJV)***

> *"We should not allow our circumstances to dictate our attitude, personality or behavior."*
> —*Yvonne M. Nelson*

Chapter 2

Saturated by His Love

The first thing I realized is that I had to release myself to God so that He could love the pain out of me. I had to let Him teach me His magnitude of love and allow His love to soak deep within my soul. This was the greatest decision I have ever made in my life! It allowed me to see that no matter what circumstances (good or bad) occur, God loves me unconditionally. He formed me in his own image. *"The Lord hath appeared of old unto me, saying, Yea I have loved thee with an everlasting love: therefore with loving kindness have I drawn thee. Again I will build thee, and thou shalt be built, O virgin of Israel: thou shalt again be adorned with thy tabrets, and shalt go forth in the dances of them that make merry" (Jer. 31:3-4 KJV).*

This relationship with God is so important. It allows us to develop a solid foundation of love, which is an essential building block to walk into the blueprint of God's design of our destiny. Once we allow His love to saturate our spirit, we are able to develop a Christlike heart and understand true love. What a great promise of hope to know that He will rebuild us from our brokenness and restore our souls and spirit with joy and peace.

Now I see myself being awake and visualizing the light of success; yet uncertain of the direction life will take to propel me again to success. *"For I know the thoughts that I think towards you, saith the Lord, thought of peace, and not of evil, to give you an expected end. Then shall ye call upon me, and ye shall go and pray unto me, and I will hearken unto you. And, ye shall seek me, and find me, when ye shall search for me with all thy heart" (Jer. 29:11-13 KJV).*

Knowing the comfort of God's plan for each of us gives us hope to see our way out of our choices, pain and sufferings. We must find hope through Christ to overcome our struggles, hurt and disappointments. Hope, by Webster's Dictionary definition, is someone or something on which expectations are centered…Intend with some possibility of fulfillment$_{(2)}$. Biblical discussions of hope reflect trust, expectation, and joyful anticipation with an absolute guarantee by the gospel's word of truth. Hope is necessary to have trust; but, without trust there is no truth. Trust is an intricate value in any of life's interactions. if we are going to form a relationship or bond, we must first trust the opportunity, *"Jesus saith unto him, I am the way, the truth, and the life: no man cometh unto the Father, but by me" (John 14:6 KJV).*

We do not have to be in despair or hopeless, because we have a God that is merciful, caring, loving and understanding of all our needs. He loves us even when we cannot love ourselves. He lifts us out of despair and brings us to safety within His arms. All of my life, I searched for love, feeling unwanted and rejected. Yet my heart was always ready to pour love into another's heart even when they were not deserving of it. Many times I cried out to God questioning His love towards me. I would always hear a small voice within saying with loving kindness "have I drawn thee?". ***"The Lord has appeared of old unto me, saying, Yea, I have loved thee with an everlasting love: Therefore with loving Kindness have I drawn thee" (Jer. 31:3 KJV).***

It's amazing how hearing God's words of comfort about His love for me still leaves me broken within my soul. Looking back on the various stages of my journey, I can see how the fragile love within me was not enough for myself or my children. I have since realized how much I have hurt my children even while trying to provide them with all of my love. My whole life I have tried to protect them from pain and disappointment, only to transfer the undercurrent of anger, frustration and pain to their spirits. Now I see and understand that my brokenness left me unable to protect them and that is so hard to accept. However, I hang on to the hope of God's love to comfort and heal us all. ***"And I will pray***

the Father, and he shall give you another Comforter, that he may abide with you forever;" (John 14:16 KJV).

The lives I have messed-up cannot be fixed by dabbing them with peroxide and watching it bubble as it attacks the bacteria. I cannot rub antibacterial cream and place gauze on them knowing that they will heal in a few days. Neither can I mix an organic potion or buy an over-the-counter medication to give them allowing them to sleep it off. There is no earthly physician who can heal them. I don't have the power of healing to transform the memories of the greatest mistakes I have imprinted on my children's hearts. All that I have is my faith, and Lord knowing, that if I stand hard and fast on this faith, He will heal us all. "***He giveth power to the faint; and to them that have no might he increaseth strength. Even the youths shall faint and be weary, and the young men shall utterly fall: But they that wait upon the Lord shall renew their strength; they shall mount up with wings as eagles; they shall run, and not be weary; and they shall walk, and not faint" (Isa. 40:29-31 KJV)***.

Where can I go to solve such a mess I have created while trying to protect my children? My love that should have provided joy, love and harmony brought confusion and pain. It hurts to see the bitter, painful journey through which my children are traveling to find themselves. Yet, I have no skill or power within my flesh to save them or protect them from all the chaos life has to offer. My only hope is to rest upon the assurance of God's promises to heal and deliver them. Thank God for His unconditional love that soothes our inner soul and brokenness. Through God we find hope, joy, encouragement and understanding of our situations. I have found that when exhaustion overtakes me and I give it to God, He begins to move and I begin to listen and follow His will. As I proceed through my journey with God's provision, I find understanding of my weakness, pain and struggles. This understanding allows me to cry out to God, my creator, who loves me unconditionally. ***"Behold I am the Lord, the God of all flesh: is there anything too hard for me?" (Jer. 32:27 KJV).***

Our ability to open our mouth in worship and cry out to God releases us into His presence and attracts His attention to us. Our personal identity is our individual sound that is birthed from our pain as we cry out to God for His mercies. It is our pain, disappointments and trials that activate our cry for God's love and attention. That is why we have to personally engage ourselves in prayer and supplication before the throne of God. We have to release ourselves with honesty and integrity before God for Him to acknowledge our humble surrender. The prayers for ourselves are for strength and spiritual covering, not the replacement of our cry to Him. The enemy's greatest control is to silence us and prevent us from crying out to God. He knows that our crying out to God, birthed out of our trials and tribulation, attracts immediate attention from our Father. So, if the enemy can silence us from crying out in worship or praying for ourselves, then our daddy God cannot hear us with urgency. *"My sheep hear my voice, I know them and they follow me: and I give them eternal life and they shall never perish, neither shall any man pluck them out of my hand" (John 10: 27-28. KJV).*

No matter how life propels us into a whirlwind, remember that God is in control. By His love, we are covered, and all that is required of us is to hold on knowing He loves us. Trusting in His everlasting love, that is pure and authentic, purifies our mind, soul and spirit. Through His love, I have grown to love and forgive myself for the damage I have inflicted on my love ones or anyone else that I have offended along my journey. I am still processing as each day unfolds, there is a new depth of pain and revelation regarding actions I may have taken along the way. I thank God for His hope, love and mercies. *"Keep yourselves in the love of God, looking for the mercy of our Lord, Jesus Christ unto eternal live" (Jude 1:21 KJV).*

How sweet it is to know we are loved even in our filthiest moments. No matter what choices we made or where we have been, He has open arms ready to love us. Knowing such love is available for us, and our only requirement is to open our hearts to receive His love, is so comforting. When we allow love to flow, only then we can begin to love ourselves and others with a Christ-like heart. Through the love of God, we can begin to flourish towards our destiny and develop the fruits of the Spirit *"I will greatly rejoice in the Lord, my soul shall be joyful in my God; for he hath clothed me with the garments of salvation, he hath covered me with the robe of righteousness, as a bridegroom decketh himself with ornaments, and as a bride adorneth herself with her jewels"* (Isa. 61:10 KJV).

> *"Our ability to open our mouth in worship and cry out to God releases us into His presence and attracts His attention to us. Our personal identity is our individual sound that is birthed from our pain as we cry out to God for His mercies. It is our pain, disappointments and trials that activate our cry for God's love and attention."*
>
> —*Yvonne M. Nelson*

Chapter 3

Surrender

Every time we leave home, we fake happiness to cover our pain. We keep ourselves busy at work to avoid feeling the pain that cuts through our souls. At the end of the day, we find our problems slapping us in the face. Our minds race, replaying all our pain, rejection and disappointments. If only we would realize the enemy's plan to keep us in bondage by sneaking in during our weakest moments, just to shatter the fragments of our mind by replaying past failures. We can't stop the enemy's designs alone. We must surrender our flesh to the will of God, along with our adversities, fears, and emotions. Then we could overthrow the enemy's stronghold. Rather than faking control, we should accept and forgive ourselves. We should accept the fact that God loves us regardless of our flaws and that we are wonderfully made in His image.

Instead, we create the illusion that we are superheroes, that we must be strong and control our emotions, fears and lives. In doing so, we only create a barrier around our hearts. As we collect the various experiences of pain, we continue to replay hopeless friendships, relationships and experiences. Which in turn only eat away at our self-esteem, inner soul and spirit, like a cancer. As a result, it takes us through a whirlwind, where we are no longer even able to fake it. We often time question whether there is a God. If He exists, why would He allow these things to happen? What we don't understand is that our fleshly choices result in adversity and despair. God is not in the mess we created, nor can He rescue us because we have detached from His covenant.

We spend our lives seeking happiness and joy in another human being who is incapable of satisfying our wants and fill the emptiness within us. How can we expect another broken vessel to fulfill our lives, when they are leaking from their inner-core?. Only God can keep the promises of life — joy and peace, and heal our brokenness. God's love is not based on our performance, for His love is undeserving and everlasting. He loves us so much that He looks beyond our faults and see our needs. He waits patiently for us to cry out for Him and His love which is unconditional. *"**There shall not any man be able to stand before thee all the days of thy life: as I was with Moses, so I will be with thee: I will not fail thee, nor forsake thee" (Josh. 1:5 KJV).**

Often times, I wonder where I went wrong with my children that made them choose the path of destruction. The damage that I have (unknowingly) done to my children has caused them to vacillate in our relationship. Their disrespect, verbal abuse, and rejection resulted in poor choices and walking away from God and His love. The pain of their choices, anger towards me, selfish treatment and rejection has left me crying out to God. I have spent sleepless nights and days crying out and clinging to the fear of being alone. How could they reject the genuine love and sacrifices I have made even in my brokenness? I had to realize that their choices are not for me to fix. Each of us has a journey that is based on the perception of our environment. We must either choose to release ourselves to the positive aspects of victory; or subject ourselves to the victim role. I had to release myself from the responsibility of the choices they made. In the end, it is left for each of us to make a conscious decision to be the change we desire to see in our lives. Regardless of my brokenness, I have always exposed them to God's word and encouraged them to be anything they desired. So, I must find comfort that with God's grace, they will go through their process and become excellent men and woman. ***"I can do all things through Christ which strengtheneth me" (Phil. 4:13. KJV).***

As I became honest with myself before God and gave Him the permission to enter my life, my healing began progressively. I began to see my brokenness and realized that my children's reaction was a result of the undercurrent of pain, rejection, frustration and generational wounds I was carrying within my spirit. There is always a root to every situation, which is passed from generation to generation. We can choose to deal honestly with our deep-rooted emotions or remain in denial. Should we choose to avoid facing our emotions, the outcome would be suffocation and a life of unfulfilled potential. Should we acknowledge, confront and surrender truthfully to ourself and God, we will begin the healing process God is capable to perform. Our commitment to present ourselves to God allows Him the opportunity to comfort and heal us. ***"But the Comforter, which is the Holy Ghost, whom the Father will send in my name, he shall teach you all things, and bring all things to your remembrance, whatsoever I have said unto you" (John 14:26 KJV).***

I finally came to terms that my life totally belongs to God. I faced my Goliath of fear, loneliness, rejection and conquered them through His promise to never leave me. I learned that God is drawn to our pain and tears in our weakest moments. I gained my strength as I surrendered to Him through my worship and praise. I allowed Him to permeate my spirit with His love and heal me. I have apologized to my children for any hurt and disappointment I have cause them because I needed to free myself from the enemy and gain victory over my destiny. I have apologized to my husband and love ones for all the hurt and injustice that I may have caused in their lives. I will never know whether they accepted my apology; but through God, I have done my part. I will forever pray for their release within their spirit, so they too can find freedom in their journey. My optimal goal is to free myself from bondage and the shackles of pain, disappointments, rejections, low self-esteem and hopelessness. *"Confess your faults one to another, and pray one for another, that ye may be healed. The effectual fervent prayer of a righteous man availeth much" (James 5: 16. KJV).*

> *"We spend our lives seeking happiness and joy in another human being who is incapable of satisfying those needs and emptiness within us. How can we expect another broken vessel to fulfill our lives when they are leaking from their inner-core?"*
>
> ***Yvonne M. Nelson***

Chapter 4

Paradigm Shift

Once I gained victory, I was able to focus on the will of God, rather than on the pain in my soul. As I began this healing, I began to see the enemy plan to consume my children and how he used my children to strip me of my hope and destiny. I made a decision that, despite how they lashed out at me, I would bombard the gates of heaven to seek God for their salvation through praying and worship. As I prayed to God for their salvation, it became clear that it was not me who had failed them; but it was their rebellious spirit against the will of God which impacted their choices.

Regardless of what life offer us, it is our choices and our reactions that determine our path. We can choose to reflect on our circumstances and use them as a light to drive us to our destiny; or we can rebel against them and focus on the flaws. However, it is natural for one to get emotionally engaged and lose focus on the blessings. When we don't count our blessings, we are left in turmoil, pain and brokenness. I finally understood that until we walk through our own trails and tribulations, we cannot understand what a relationship with God is. ***"And the prayer of the faith shall save the sick, and the Lord shall raise him up; and if he have committed sins, they shall be forgiven him" (James 5: 15. KJV).***

Our intentions and our purposes have to coincide and be made part of our subconsciousness. We are then able to develop a sense of direction which allows us to venture to our destiny through faith. This faith allows us to gain confidence to step out from our familiar practices to the unfamiliar calling of God. "Now f***aith is the substance of things hope for, the evidence of things not seen" (Heb. 11:1. KJV).*** Once we are able to function on the unfamiliar and set our life to move freely in God's will; everything within us will be aligned to a greater level of integrity. Then, our authenticity will evolve allowing us to acknowledge our fear, flaws, and weaknesses. Then, we will be able to confront and unmask our secret rejections. The enemy has lost, and we have gained the victory to walk in the promises of God to their fullest. Our obstacles and trials will take a different direction and will propel us into our destiny. Because now we can reflect upon our trials positively and speak life into our destiny.

I have been meditating and revisiting my blessings and how awesome God has been to me. I cannot even begin to express His grace and mercy through the seasons of disappointment, regret and pain. However,

God's mercies are revealed when I revisit those seasons. I have wondered many times whether there is a God during my struggles and pain. Today, I know He has never changed or left me; it was I who had changed and left to fill the emptiness within my soul by chasing fleshly desires. **" ...I will never leave thee nor forsake thee" (Heb. 13:5, KJV).**

It was God who possessed my reins and created all the inner complex parts of my body within my mother's womb with such marvelous workmanship. He choose me with His love within my mother's womb, recording every second of my life in His precious thoughts, despite my imperfection. As the psalmist stated, if he was to count the thoughts of God towards him they would outnumber the grains of sand (**Ps. 139:18 KJV**). God's love allows us to recognize our feelings of anger, envy, resentment, prejudice and hate within our soul. His love helps us to realize that we have to be redirected and understood if we are to avoid the vicious circle of life that suffocates and poisons us and the universe.

The very walls that we build to protect ourselves from hurt, disappointments and others are the very walls that prevent us from reaching our full potential. They deter our blessings and prevent us from experiencing prosperity and happiness. It is these walls that strip us of self-esteem and project the spirit of rejection that consumes us. They prevent us from finding hope in anything or anyone that we interact with daily. Paulo Freire stated " Without hope there is no future." Therefore, hope is one of the ingredients necessary to navigate our journey through our struggles. Paulo Freire goes on to explain that without hope we move into hopelessness; which in turn leaves us as hopeless and despairing individuals. As a results our struggles, we will become suicidal.*(3)*

Hope in God provides light in our darkest moments. It is the pivotal moment of strength, when we are weak and distorted with no sense of understanding or direction. When our lives are in rage, tossing us from all angles, and we don't even have the strength to stand or look up. We are lost, confused and blinded. No one is there to give a word of encouragement, direction or provision. We are left to either hold onto the memories of our spiritual knowledge, or try to pull ourselves out using our own strength. I thank God for the word that was written within my soul as a child, as it was those words that provided me the light of hope to fight through my struggles. ***"Thy word is a lamp unto my feet, and a light unto my path" (Ps. 119:105, KJV).***

When an individual is able to surrender to the hope of faith, it provides them a way to hold on and push themself toward the light of God. We learn to lean, not on our own understanding; but instead we lean towards the word of God. That is why it is important to be honest with our feelings of anger, pain, and disappointments.

When we touch the core of those feelings, we are able to surrender them as we propel toward our journey to healing, with hope to gain freedom from oppression. This will allow us to grow to our full potential.

I praise Him today for: His love even when I could not love myself; His patience while teaching me patience' His kindness and strength when I felt my weakness (as others took advantage of me); His joy that was overshadowed because many misunderstood me; His peace that I have learned to find comfort in; and, most of all, for choosing me for His salvation. *"And even to your old age I am he; and even to hoar hairs will I carry you.: I have made, and I will bear; even I will carry, and will deliver you" (Isa. 46:4 KJV).*

Even though my life is still shifting, I find comfort within that gives me reassurance all will be well. I feel a new journey has begun in His presence that is filled with destiny even though I am clueless of how it will evolve. I am beginning to open up to a new world that will allow me to begin reassessing and redefining who I am. Doctrines and values that have driven me to this point must be revised. Some values may be discarded or upgraded to accelerate growth towards my destiny.

Often times, life take us to a place where we lose our ability to achieve and our emotions respond with fear, anxiety, apathy, boredom and low self-esteem. We then loose our self-respect and begin to wrestle with perfectionism and our ego. it is during the process of wrestling with perfectionism and our ego that our motivation falls low. We need to find a balance by renewing our minds and evaluating our goals in life. We need to realize that within every failure is found the seed to our success. There is no such things as failure, but only feedback which motivates us to regain our momentum.

The first step is to exam our goals and their importance and then decide what we are willing to sacrifice in the process. Our goals are the desired outcome to learn and develop consistency. Everything else we encounter on the way to accomplishing these goals provides feedback, helping us to mature. We should set goals that are specific and targeted towards our desired outcome. They should be measurable, align to our values, realistic and given a time line.

Step two is to recognize and identify the root of our fear deep in our core. Changes in our core are mandatory and will be reflected in our lives. Therefore, we must face the giant deep within to acquire understanding of its origin. Fear, often time, paralyzes our confidence and prevents us from achieving our goals. One has to conquer the spirit of fear to regain confidence within their emotional wellbeing. The pursuit of success moves us into position and evokes our ownership of the future. Every individual is responsible for everything that they think, say or feel. It is necessary to recognize that ownership to be master.

The third step is to deal with self in its most primitive state which is our ego. Our ego reflects our pride which give the feeling of superiority. The ego in one of the challenges human beings have to conquer. It fosters such arrogance that it allows us to be self- righteous and judgmental in our relationships or interactions with people and God. If one does not check their ego, it can become a stumbling block in every aspect of life. It develops into pride which interferes with our personal and spiritual walk. The trick is we believe we are always right and no one can tell us anything. A self-righteous attitude places us in a know-it-all disposition. This impedes our ability to form relationships in every aspect of life. As a result, relationships are often times abandoned and submission becomes difficult to life circumstance or the will of God. *"Pride goeth before destruction, and an haughty spirit before a fall. Better it is to be of a humble spirit with the lowly, than to divide the spoil with the proud" (Prov. 16:18-19, KJV).*

Achieving these simple steps allows us to open ourselves to receive life. When we encounter another, the need to defend, divide and conquer no longer becomes the first response. Each experience is evaluated for its actual worth. This allows us to be free to receive wisdom and knowledge. Once this is accomplished, we can live life at its optimal level because we shifted our achievements and motivation to high gear. Our energy is now refocused to a positive desired outcome as a result of our ability to freely accept the experience in its raw state.

> *"We need to realize that within every failure is found the seed to our success because there is no such thing as failure; but only feedback, which motivate us to regain our momentum."*
> *Yvonne M. Nelson*

CHAPTER 5

Silence

Learning to be silent has been a lesson that I have been learning on so many levels (spiritually, emotionally, physically and worldly). These last thirteen years of my life, I became silent due to disappointments, pain, feelings of hopelessness, and patiently waiting on God to provide a solution. This season allows me to watch God's unfolding hands within my life.

Silence by definition of Webster's Dictionary is the absence of sound or noise.$_{(2)}$ Silence may also refer to any absence of communication whether negative or positive, depending on the cultural norms. Silence can also be used as total communion in reference to non-verbal communication and spiritual connection.

I remember beginning the journey broken, hurt and feeling so defeated in every aspect of my life. I had no one to talk with, as friends were very limited and family turned their backs on me out of disappointment regarding my decisions. Often times I wondered where everyone was when I needed them; and why I was always there for them in their times of need. I was in a place of wondering if God was even there for me, and why He would allow such devastation and unfairness to occur in my life.

Often times our hurt comes from one that knows us or has a relationship with us. It's those that know our deep thoughts, sleep and play with us, and know our character who often time are cruel towards us. However, I have found that the greater the anointing the greater the struggle. Anointing will cause tears, cost relationships, friendships, emotions, strength and energy. Anointing and God's favor will bring us to a place of disappointment in others in their behavior towards God's children.

In such a dark place, we can only sit still and reach out for the one thing that gives hope and life, which is God. The weight of life bears heavy; but the breath of hope will help us survive and see the light again. Silence in these dark times teaches us to reach deep within every stitch of our soul and mind pressing to the light. It is amazing how these dark moments draw us like magnets towards the glory of God. Our ears are tuned to every channel, learning the voice of God. Our eyes are like eagles to see God's words as foot prints towards our deliverance.

Through these warfare experiences, God's words begin to take root within my heart, spirit and life. God's words begin preserving me through His grace and mercies. Often times, death occupies my mind and soul; but God has been so real and good to me. I could have been dead in my grave; but God told death to stand back and release me. I cling to the promise given to me in my dream when Jesus, in the Garden of Gethsemane, touched my head and told me His grace will be sufficient to carry me through this journey. However, the weight of life sometimes beats me down while clinging to His promises. *"Be strong and of good courage, fear not, nor be afraid of them: for the Lord thy God, he is that doth go with thee;. He will not fail thee, nor forsake thee" (Deut. 31:6 KJV).*

Often, I sit and cry through my feelings of hopelessness but; out of nowhere God's spirit wraps me in His arms of comfort. Tragic and uncommon places brought me to feast on the words of God; often questioning if it will ever end or if it is my life's journey. His words of maximum grace gives me hope during the greatness of my darkness. I heard myself saying "Philippians 4" clearly as I awoke one morning. I quickly came to realize that it was a provision from God for my journey ahead. After reading the entire chapter, I discovered, if I believe that the safest place would be the Master's arm, then my battles would not be fought alone. Although many experiences have left me trying to console myself, the tears brought healing to my deepest pain and inner being.

Today, silence brings a new meaning to my spirit. It is a means to hear the gentle voice of the Holy Spirit as it confirms or convicts me regarding the relationship with my Father and creator. It is a time for me to learn stillness and patience for the desired outcome. It is a time for reflection; thus allowing me to reorganize my mind, soul and spirit toward God. ***"Be still, and know that I am Lord…." (Ps. 46:10 KJV).*** It is an art everyone has to learn if we are going to hear God's quiet voice on the tip of our ears. ***"And they heard the voice of the Lord God walking in the Garden in the cool of the day: …" (Gen. 3:8 KJV).*** It is quite clear that there cannot be noise and confusion if we are to hear the voice of the Lord clearly.

There is great reward should we learn to purposely quiet ourselves from the external and internal impulses that propel us in motion. This stillness allows us to hear the quiet voice of our Master speaking to our soul and spirit, redirecting us if need be. Should we learn to master control of our mind, the enemy would not have the privilege to torment us with the constant replay of our issues. The battle would not be ours, it would truly belong to God. ***"My sheep hear my voice, and I know them, and they will follow me" (John 10:27 KJV).***

Silence no longer makes me uncomfortable when life begins to twirl, as I have learned that it is within those moments God sprinkles life within my spirit. I earnestly seek silence in any moment of turmoil that attempts to consume me so I can hear the voice of God minister to my spirit. Such solitude with God is more rewarding than consulting with people who have nothing to offer but misdirection and nonconstructive criticism, reflecting their own fleshly and broken spirit.

Silence allows us to spend time in His word and His presence crying out to Him; allowing Him to stir-up issues within us and deliver us from our pain, rejection and ungodly emotions. It is a means to rejuvenate our soul and spirit. These quiet moments allow us to see the strength of God at work inside of us, even when it appears impossible to the human intellect and emotions. *"For with God nothing shall be impossible"(Luke 1:37 KJV).*

> *'There is great reward should we learn to purposely quiet ourselves from the external and internal impulses that propel us in motion. This stillness allows us to hear the quiet voice of our Master speaking to our soul and spirit, redirecting us if need be."*
>
> *Yvonne M. Nelson*

Chapter 6

Dark Season

Everyone, at one time or another, has experienced a dark season or a wilderness experience. It is a time when all that can go wrong is occurring and it appears that all our friends, family, and loved ones have vanished from our presence. This season of our life forces us to face our inner core and draw from our spiritual beliefs. It is also a season when we can drown in feelings of hopelessness, solitude and depression. We find ourselves in a place of desolate silence and we enter the battle field of our minds and spirit.

This season of darkness takes us to a place that gives the enemy permission to bombard our minds. He will replay every broken dream, hurt, disappointment and failure that has shattered our self-esteem. Every negative thought spoken into our situation or life provides the enemy with the equipment or tools to conquer us. The constant bombardment of negative thoughts will leave us fragile and shattered to pieces. In this season, we are challenged spiritually between good or evil, and the human yearning to be connected with something larger than our egos. ***"Be sober, be vigilant, because your adversary the devil, as a roaring lion, walked about seeking whom he may devour" (1 Pet. 5:8 KJV).***

Webster defines the ego as the "I" or self of any person$_{(2)}$ (ego is Latin for "I"). In psychological terms, the ego is the part of the psyche that experiences the outside world and reacts to it. It comes between the primitive drive of the id and the demands of the social environment, represented by the superego. ***"I can of mine own self do nothing: as I hear, I judge: and my judgement is just; because I seek not mine own will, but the will of the father which has sent me" (John 5:30 KJV).***

When we find ourselves in the grip of something larger than society's expectation or the ego's need, we enter into our spiritual crises. We find ourselves struggling between our ego (pride) and surrendering to something larger. The ego often times become frustrated within itself and its lack of control, inefficient performance, poor choices and uncontrollable outcomes that spiral out of control. Life eventually turns into an uncontrolled and unpredictable roller coaster ride. Our ego struggles to prevent us from humbling ourselves which delays the opportunity to be healed. ***"The wicked, through the pride of his countenance will not seek after God: God is not in all his thoughts" (Ps. 10:4 KJV).***

Our comatose spirit is being stirred and shifted during this dark season. This leaves us with a feeling of uneasiness. We are unable to see the blessings as we focus on the disappointments and pain. Drowning in our insecurities will manifest or create an enlargement of our circumstances. We become so blind that we cannot even understand God's gracious love or His covenant in the mist of our mess. The moment we are rocked to our core and broken within our soul, we miraculously discover there is a God in our life upon Whom we can call. ***"Call unto me, and I will answer thee, and show thee great and unsearchable things you do not know" (Jer. 33:3 KJV).***

Why does it take a crisis in our lives or to be totally broken in spirit, to discover who God is? God has never left us, He has been there all the time with open arms. Rather, we have left Him for our fleshly desires. We rested on our own strength forgetting about Him and believing our ego. However, with open arms and His love, God remains patient, waiting for us to return home. We often return home still trying to hold on to our fleshly desires. We try to bargain with God with promises in turn for our deliverance. Yet, when our lives are restored and our crisis is over, we forget the commitments we promised to God while calling for help.

Our dark season of problems, failures, weakness and neediness allows us to see the light of God, should we decide to rely on Him rather than our own strength. These moments are designed to awaken a new dimension of resources and teach us humility before our Father. Then God can catapult us to a new spiritual and physical level that will ignite our faith in a new and fresh journey. It's a means to invoke and evoke in us our full capacity towards our destiny designed by God.

Allowing God to be our companion brings a lightness to our steps, our trials, and our tribulations. Developing a relationship with God provides us the opportunity to cling to His presence which brings us peace in the mist of our adversity. Once we learn to deny our fleshly desires and invite the presence of God to enter our thoughts, spirit and body; we will begin to truly rely on Him. As we allow ourselves to rely on God, we will develop a loving relationship with Him so His will become the Navigator of our daily tasks. We will be able to receive the reciprocal process of love deep within us; that brings change into our soul, spirit and physical being. *"... That ye should shew forth the praises of him who hath called you out of darkness into his marvelous light" (1 Pet. 2:9 KJV).*

It's easier-said-than-done when everything is falling apart and we still haven't found the answer for the first step. During that time, every angle in our life will be dark with limited light to provide any hope. The battlefield within the mind will intensify as our spirit struggles. We may become isolated, having no one to turn to or talk with, mostly because of our shame, behavior, embarrassment and disappointment. One of the devil's plan is to capture us in darkness to win our soul from God. Isolation makes us weak and prevents us from finding solutions in a world of darkness and chaos. It convinces us that everyone and everything in life is against us and we begin to play the victim role and lose the battle of hope.

When life tosses us into a whirlwind, we grab at anything that gives hope. Somewhere in the mist of confusion we begin to seek the God of the universe. Church becomes a place to seek answers and hope. However, we often leave the same way we enter, at a loss for solutions. The institution (church) lacks insight due to its own agenda or formality. Sometimes, the moment of failed connections leaves us with the feeling of disappointment, loneliness and hurt (adding to our existing ones). Our desperate cry for an opportunity to talk with leadership, or a word of hope and direction, are often times shattered.

My dark season has been a process of finding my way. It was a desolate place with feelings of loneliness and nowhere to turn. Every direction brought a wall too high to climb. Friends and family were nowhere to be found; thus I lacked support. I grabbed onto faith and trust to move forward, only to find the solution failed. I was beaten down emotionally, spiritually and physically as I was failing in my finances, my job, and my family. It is like being in a pit or in the wilderness. It's a place of Lo debar (a low in place) with no connection to society and the lack of desire to continue. This lo debar place leaves us hopeless to even find the strength to pray and cry out to the Father.

Wilderness represents any desolate, barren or unpopulated area. *Webster dictionary defines wilderness as a wild and uninhabited area left in its natural condition (2).* When we look throughout the Bible in every wilderness situation, God was always present. *Exodus 3:18 ...Let us go, we beseech thee, three days' journey into the wilderness, that we may sacrifice to the Lord our God. Numbers 14:2 "....If only we had died in Egypt, or even here in the wilderness!: they complained". Deuteronomy 1:19 "Then just as the Lord our God directed us, we left Mount Sinai and traveled through the great and terrifying wilderness ...". Matthew 3:3 "The voice of one crying in the wilderness: Prepare ye the way of the Lord, Make his path straight". Matthew 4:1 "Then Jesus was led up of the spirit into the wilderness to be tempted of the Devil." (KJV).*

It is quite clear that the wilderness, or dark season, in our lives is a process to prune us from our fleshly desires and self. A season that allow us to be stripped of our pride, ego and self-dependency and provides strength which pushes us to find God's face. It is definitely a time when we will learn to surrender and allow God to mold us into His image.

The wilderness provides time when we submit to God's hands shaping us. This dark season allows us to find our *stride*, *" faith "* and begin a journey in learning God's voice. You see ***"Faith is the substance of things hoped for, the evidence of things not seen" (Heb. 11:1 KJV).*** Should we read further, ***" But without faith it is impossible to please him: for he that cometh to God must believe that he is, and that he is a rewarder of them that diligently seek him" (Heb. 11:6 KJV).***

Our dark season will last until we find our *stride*" *faith*" and understand its full potential in our spiritual life. Faith will not be learned immediately; but, each time we go through difficult moments, we will learn to embrace with strength to trust and believe that God is in control. It is our daily dying to the flesh that kills the ego that cultivates our pride. Every trial throughout our life allows us to grow spiritually in our faith and brings us closer to stripping our ego, so we can become stronger in our walk. Only when we learn to master our faith walk, will we begin to gain strength to propel us through each and every struggle with His grace and mercy as the wind behind our back.

It is quite clear that the wilderness or dark season in our lives is a process to prune us from our fleshly desires and self. A season that allow us to be stripped of our pride, ego and self-dependency and provides strength which pushes us to find God's face. It is definitely a time when we will learn to surrender and allow God to mold us into his image.

Yvonne M. Nelson

Chapter 7

The Spirit of Oppression

It is common among us to live pretending to our peers, family and friends that all is well in our lives. The truth is we are walking around with unforgiven grudges, holding on to hurt, pain, disappointments, rejection and low self-esteem. We have learned to "stuff" our emotions deep into our subconscious instead of facing and dealing with them. We learn to display the face that is appropriate to the environment or situation we are confronted with on a daily basis. We allow ourselves to become a reservoir holding "stuff" that becomes toxic to us and keeps us in bondage. Everyone with whom we interact can see the pain and frustration within us which we work so hard to cover up. We portray a life of happiness while struggling to maintain our sanity.

Are you one of those people? Have you experienced feelings and emotions that have been too painful to deal with each time they surfaced? Have your experiences or relationships brought you to a place of mistrust that caused you to be frustrated or replay the painful experiences? How many times do you smile and pretend life is great while inside you are dying from loneliness, pain and grief? Do you find yourself continually telling God, "I am not ready yet, Lord!" Do you find yourself keeping busy or hiding behind the word of God? Do you convince yourself that all you need in life is God and no one else? (I will address that problem later.) Well, it is time for us to free ourselves from our oppression.

Oppression brings to our mind the thought of slavery, or someone keeping us from succeeding. We play victim through life blaming others and denying the problem. We refuse to take ownership of our problems because denial is a comfortable place that allow us to survive the storm. However, no matter what our choices are, the problems remain our struggles until we face and own them. By Webster's definition "oppression is a state of force or authority. *Oppression is any unjust or cruel exercise of authority or power; a sense of being weighed down in body and mind. To be oppress is to be crush or burden by abuse of power or authority; to be burden spiritually or mentally"*$_{(2)}$. So it is quite clear that oppression comes in many forms and shapes.

Oppression can be reflected in our: finances; lack of self-esteem; emotional, physical or sexual abuse; marriage; struggles with our children or loved ones; reliance on alcohol; lack of love; or anything that weighs us down. In order for us to gain freedom from our oppression, we must first release the oppressive situation and give ourselves the permission to move on. The author ***Maxine Green, states "Freedom must be achieved through continuous resistance to the forces that limit, condition, determine and too frequently oppress us." She continues to explain that one will only reach their maturity when they can view their experiences as a reflection and utilizes them as a stepping stone to move on to higher levels".(4).*** The fact is, life may not have offered us the greatest experiences, but we must make a choice through how we handle it and aim to be the best we can be.

We must first come to the realization that we are in bondage and face the giant within. Once we come to terms, face the giants in our lives, and stop blaming others for our misfortune, the journey to freedom will begin. Therefore, if we are going to release ourselves from our oppressor, then we have to acknowledge the things that are oppressing us. There is a root to every situation that will continue to replay and impact us in a negative way. Many times, the devil will channel our thoughts and emotions to deal with only the branches. However, these branches will continue to grow should we continue to rehearse our painful negative experiences.

Our stories become alive within our mind, soul, spirit, and reality. The script becomes intense and develops into a monster that over-powers our soul, mind and spirit. We begin to live a life in solitude as a means of protecting ourself from pain, disappointment and others. When we isolate, we limit our social skills, create loneliness and create a world of unhappiness. We live a life of existence rather than a life of purpose. This place of solitude becomes comfortable, safe and complacent to us. When, in fact it, is a place that robs us of our true joy, fulfillment in life, and limits God's desires and destiny for us. It creates a life of struggles and pain which we were never meant to encounter. It brings along depression that creates division, isolation and loneliness, which can lead to suicidal ideations and self-destructive behaviors.

In other words, our oppression is deep rooted in our experiences. We can make a choice to deal honestly with them or remain in denial by putting makeup on them. We can hide behind self-destructive behaviors such as drugs, alcohol, self-infliction to our bodies or other inappropriate behaviors. The result will be that we will continue to "stuff" these experiences into our grocery bag and drag them along from one life experience or relationship to another. Whenever familiar circumstances appear before us, our first response is to dig into our grocery bag and replay the old experience with our new one. However, when we deal honestly with ourselves, we can become free and leave our bags behind at the dumpsite. If we are honest and truthful to ourselves and God it allows Him to heal our wounds. *"and ye shall know the truth and the truth shall make you free" (John 8:32 KJV).*

Life's experiences have placed our mindset, soul and spirit in opposition which runs deep within our soul. Rejection develops the spirit of fear, and fear controls our emotions which can interfere with our experience of God. Fear dominates our thoughts, emotion, hope and even our faith throughout our life. Many times, it limits our faith in God's ability to fulfill our destiny. Fear is the enemy that destroys, directs, divides and conquers life for us. The God we serve has authority over our lives and also provides us the choice of life and death in our tongue. Rehearsing our struggles, rehashing the pain and clinging to the pain, allows the enemy to dig his claws within our soul and rob us from all that God has for us. *"What shall we then say to these things? If God be for us, who can be against us?" (Rom. 8:31 KJV).*

It is to our advantage to give God permission to purge our emotion and physical pain. This will allow His healing balm to saturate our soul deeper than we can ever imagine. Resisting to let go our pain and open ourselves to what life has each day limits God's hand within our destiny. If we continue to hold on to those struggles, we control our interaction to avoid disappointment, hurt or reaching our full potential in serving the God we worship. Life becomes stagnate and pollutes our soul and true relationship to God. We only allow God to give us a half glass when we use comfort controlling practices in life.

Forgiveness is the next and greatest test when opening the door to our deliverance. Not just forgiveness to the offender, but also the ability to forgive oneself. Often, we crucify ourselves by not forgiving ourselves. God has forgiven us, but we continue to punish ourselves for our mistakes or choices leaving us to miss out on our full potential. *Forgiveness by Webster's Dictionary "is to give up resentment against the offender."*[2] So, letting go our feelings of anger towards anyone that has hurt us is the ultimate goal when unburdening our heart.

Holding on to our history of pain and resentment only costs us the fulfillment of our destiny. If the truth be told, those that have offended us have moved on without any knowledge of their action. They have been victims within their own story. Therefore, holding on to their actions and refusing to forgive them only affects our soul. The time spent replaying negative memories only leads to the withdrawal of our energy towards our destination.

The more we rehearse the vision of the actions that caused us pain, we affect our emotions and create idols of history that dominate our life. So, forgiveness is a gift to give to ourselves as it allows us to release ourselves from the perpetrators rather than exonerating them.

Forgiveness expresses our strength so they have no control over us. Forgiveness allows us to move on from the offense that once controlled our thoughts, actions and outcome. Then we are able to release ourselves by rerouting our thoughts about our oppressors. Being able to release them allows us sight to see through the eyes of God, that they are also His children and just as hurt as we are.

We all have fallen short of God's glory. We desire His forgiveness so we have a chance to enter the kingdom of God. How can we have the audacity to receive forgiveness for those we hurt or even request forgiveness from God. This mentality is double minded in the sight of God and ourselves. When we are not able to forgive those that offended us we have robbed ourselves of our freedom to return home to the Father in heaven. Then Peter came and said to him, ***"Lord, how often shall my brother sin against me and I forgive him? Till seven times? Jesus said unto him, I say not unto thee, until seven times: but, until seventy times seven" (Matt. 18: 20-22 KJV).***

Once we learn how to forgive our oppressors, we have to reciprocate our love towards all that have caused our pain. Loving them does not mean you are subjected to their perpetuating behaviors. Loving them for your freedom is the utmost result of such actions. In order for us to reciprocate love, we have to open our hearts to loving others. It is easier to love those that treat us kindly than it is to love those who offend us. We cannot allow someone that is dysfunctional to dictate our destiny or behavior. God requires us to love others as we love ourselves. It is difficult for us to love others that are offensive to us. However, when we are able to love ourselves, and live for the promises of God, we are able to love those that offend us with a heart of Christ. ***"Thou shall love the lord thy God with all thy heart, and with all thy soul and with all thy mind."*** Second commandment is to*"**... love thy neighbor as thy self" (Matt. 22: 37-40 KJV).*** It would be accurate to say if we choose to live by God's principles, we are to love others with no contingency. True commitment to God is a guarantee when we release our oppressors and allow God's love to overflow into our lives. We should all thrive to seek and focus on God's word, building a relationship with Him and accepting His presence into our lives to the fullest. We will experience His healing, restoration, peace and joy deep within our soul as we allow ourselves to flourish toward the love of God.

> *In other words, our oppression is deep rooted in our experiences. We can make a choice to deal honestly with them or remain in denial by putting makeup on them. We can hide behind self-destructive behaviors of drugs, alcohol, self-infliction to our bodies or inappropriate behaviors. The result will be that*

we will continue to "stuff' these experiences into our grocery bag and drag them along from one life experience or relationship to another.

Yvonne M. Nelson

Chapter 8

Deliverance

There comes a point where something inside of us draws a line against our deep inner fears, hurts and bondages. We stand on the premise that God has given us power and deliverance from our struggles. The enemy cannot go any further than we allow him. Should we surrender in total submission in Christ and stand on His words, we would embark on our journey of healing. ***"Ye are of God, little children, and have overcome them: because greater is he that is in you than he that is in the world" (1 John 4:4 KJV).*** The moment we stop mimicking the words and move to the level of believing and living, our thoughts and communication process with others also moves to another level.

The enemy's greatest fear is that we are going to rise up with surrendered worship to God and step back into His glory with something of heaven on our hearts. As long as the enemy stops us from worshiping God, we are not a threat to him. So if we surrender our pain in worship and prayers we release the stronghold of the enemy from our lives. When we are able to transform our thoughts of defeat into the hope and presence of God, we awaken within our soul a fight.

Life vacillates when we allow ourselves to be bound by routines that hinder our growth, direction and destiny God has prepared for us. Changes bring us in the promises of God. When we allow God to attach Himself to us, and we in turn surrender to His will, then we have given Him permission to direct us through our storms towards our destiny. Once we have accomplished total submission, God is able to process us through our trials and tribulations, that will in turn lead us towards our destiny to receive the blessings He has already prepared for us. However, when we take control of our life, we have placed blinders on our eyes and create a life of chaos that hinders our destiny and blessings. ***"He that dwelleth in the secret place of the most high shall abide under the shadow of the Almighty" (Ps. 91:1 KJV).***

Our hearts know the bitterness or bitter roots buried deep within our subconscious mind. As a result, we refuse to work through and are left paralyzed as it eats at our inner core like cancer. It's a process that never ceases and our blessings and character is consumed by the seconds of the day. We are not even capable to imagine ourselves blessed or worthy of success. Some are able to rise in fortune, fame and wealth but inner peace is never attained at the end of the day due to unfinished emotions buried within their soul.

The final outcome that we often deal with before closing our eyes is the emptiness of our hearts that cry louder than our voice could ever propel. The greatest step that we could ever take to break this vicious disease is forgiveness to the one that offended or hurt us in any shape or fashion. Yet it is the hardest thing for an individual to accomplish because of our pride. If we could understand that the overall benefit of forgiveness is more for us, then we could easily embrace the idea. ***"For if ye forgive men their trespasses, your heavenly Father will also forgive you. But if you forgive not men their trespasses neither will your Father forgive your trespasses" (Matt. 6: 14-15 KJV).***

It is natural for humans to harbor dislike towards someone that has hurt them, acted wrong towards them or has treated them unfairly. The longer we meditate on those feelings, we become bitter and angry, then they become stronger and overpower our spirits. In the long run, these feelings of hate grow and destroys any hope of happiness life has for us. The saddest outcome is we pass this toxic undercurrent from generation to generation though our offspring. Our joy, peace and abundant of life is robbed daily from us. God's plan for us is to live life abundantly can never become a reality due our cluttered emotions.

Our coping mechanism provides a survival mode to carry us through the storms of life. However, if we are not careful we get consumed, become complacent, and develop dysfunctional life styles. Often time these life styles lock us within ourselves until we become numb to our feelings. It is important for us to redirect our thoughts and emotions throughout life, as it allows us to make changes in our behavior or habits. As we are able to adjust our thought process, we are able to reflect on the pain within and hopefully decide to release it. This freedom comes with God's request for us to forgive one another as He forgave us. ***"Forbearing one another, and forgiving one another, If any man have a quarrel against any: even as Christ forgave you, so also do ye" (Col. 3:13 KJV).***

Forgiveness is between God and ourselves, not the offender. Forgiveness is required by God. Our eternal life depends on it. So, the quicker we release the hurt to God by asking Him to forgive the offender and remove the hurt from within us, His holy spirit will flow through us. We will begin to feel His sweet peace flowing through us melting away the anger and bitterness within us and towards the offender. Once we let go and forgive as Christ forgave the thief on the cross beside Him, we will be able to challenge and conquer our greatest giants from within. Once we free ourselves of the pain and toxicity, God is able to pour the love that heals our soul and birth His desires to do His will within us. ***"Judge not, and ye shall not be judge: condemn not,***

and ye shall not be condemned: forgive, and ye shall be forgiven" (Luke 6:37 KJV).

Ah, but we spend our life savoring the sweet bitterness of our experiences daily, as if it was some valuable heirloom. As a result, we miss every opportunity for blessings, relationship, family. We miss the ability to tap into our talents, gifts or our full potential that God presents to us in one form or another throughout our lives. We create a world of turmoil and wasted energy on what happened, rather than what should happen. We keep ourselves busy and hide behind our work, meeting other's needs, religious and cultural practices, and fear. As a result, we fail to identify the ideas or opportunities that would prosper or propel us into our destiny, or even develop us into our full capacity within society. Holding resentment within our soul also blocks the hand of God from blessing our emotional spiritual space. We spend wasted years waiting on God to move while God is waiting for us to purge ourselves, and allow Him to enter our spirit. It is only at the end of life some figure it out with deepest regrets, with no time to regain anything. While others go to rest in peace with no insight into their choices. " ***Wisdom is the principal thing; therefore get wisdom: and with all thy getting get understanding" (Prov. 4:7 KJV).***

First, we need to realize that the greatest person to forgive is ourselves of every failure or poor choice we have made in life. This gives us power against the enemy, within the battlefield of our mind. Second, we should release our offenders through prayer and forgiveness. This allows freedom in our inner soul and spirit that allows God to dwell within us. Our freedom provides us an experience of peace within our soul that passes all understanding. God has already bought and paid the price for our failures and mistakes, so why not walk into our destiny courageously free. The ultimate lesson in life that is so important is not what we experience, but how we respond to our oppositions. Our response is the ultimate decision of whether we remain trapped or we begin our deliverance process ***"Nay, in all these things we are more than conquerors through him that loved us. For I am persuaded, that death, nor life, nor angels, nor principalities, nor powers, nor things present, nor things to come, nor height, nor depth, nor any other creature, shall be able to separate us from the love of God, which is in Christ Jesus our Lord" (Rom. 8: 37-39 KJV).***

The story of the prodigal son was more than just a boy returning home to his father. It was about the unconditional love of the father to celebrate his lost child returning home. The real message was the heart of the father who forgave his son and welcomed him with open arms and poured out his love. If this human father is able to receive his son whole heartily with love, how much more will our Father in heaven receive us? That

Christ-like heart the father demonstrated through his love began to break any spirit of rejection that could have affected his son's life. God Himself celebrates each time one of us return home because He said He will leave the ninety nine and seek the one sheep that is lost. That is how important our lives are to God. That is why He sent His one and only son to give us eternal life. ***"What man of you, having a hundred sheep, if he lose one of them, doth not leave the ninety and nine in the wilderness, and go after that which is lost, until he find it?" (Luke 15:4 KJV).***

We all are a reflection of the prodigal son. All of us have experienced different journeys that left us with misconstrued perceptions. As a result, we have encountered some bitter and painful experiences that have resulted in poor choices in life. Through the process of evolving through these experiences, we begin to create our believes into stories that impact our spirit deeply. Our private stories are what we create within us about failures, low self-esteem, being unloved, rejection and the list goes on. These beliefs begin to drive us deeper as we rehearse them daily, and become real in our soul and spirit.

The enemy capitalizes on our beliefs and holds us ransom through the stories that we have written for ourselves. These stories create defensive feelings and frustration that project strife in our families, friends and love ones. These feelings create a toxic poison in our souls and over-shadow you spiritually, morally, and ethically. We become out of control bringing us to a lonely place; thus giving the enemy greater control of our mind, soul and emotions. The truth be told, if we could begin to forgive ourselves and others we would be able to see the light. God gave His son for us so that we could be forgiven; yet we spend our time finding reason not to forgive ourselves and others, by beating ourselves daily about our poor choices or what someone has done to us. ***"Thy word is a lamp unto my feet, and a light unto my path" (Ps. 119: 105 KJV).***

Often times, our journey brings within us pain, hardship, trials, rejections and unlimited stumbling blocks. If we could only find the strength to look within ourselves, own and embrace our pain, we could find the steps home. When we are able to own our pain and disappointments, it opens a new door of vision and hope within our life. It allows us to begin a journey toward our designed destiny. Whether we take the scenic route or the direct path is not the issue. We need to know that these experiences push us towards our inner core that propels our faith. These testimonies allow our bodies to become sensitive to all the misconstrued experiences, and allow us to touch the emotions deep within our soul. As we take that step of faith to begin the process within ourselves, we will find the strength to press our way towards God. This process allows us to change our stories and forgive ourselves allowing us to return home to our Father. *"He heals the broken in heart, and bindeth up their wounds" (Ps. 147:3 KJV).*

Often, after we return home, shame and condemnation approaches us to convince us that we are unworthy, but that is far from the truth. The enemy will rise up and replay our stories which propel us into the battlefield of the mind. The thing that is important for us to give ourselves and God is permission to address each level of pain, disappointments, hate, low self-esteem, pride, shackles of failure, and oppressions that have buried us throughout our lives. Pour out our basket of toxins and touch every emotion connected to them within every strand of our body, mind and soul. Find our shoes (hope) and learn to walk in them through faith, forgiveness and love, taking the leap of faith. *Hebrew 11 clearly discusses the importance of our faith in God...how by faith Abel, Noah, Enoch etc.. received the approval of God. "But without faith It is impossible to please him: For he that cometh to God must believe that he is, and that he is rewarder of them that diligently seek him" (Heb. 11:6 KJV).*

So as a child of God, walk in peace and love, allowing yourself to be healed taking on the countenance that if God is for us, who can be against us. Leap into transformation which allows God to peel away the layers of darkness, exposing our core being, while touching our true emotions. Our core, the center of our soul, is the most important part as it directs our destiny. Our core is what develop us into our purpose, success and helps define our prospective view of ourselves and life. It contributes to our immediate gratification, building lasting relationships, trusting others and provides us the freedom to receive opportunities for what they are worth.

Our core will always direct us if we nurture it with great choices, process positive thoughts, and ultimate positioning in a nurturing environment. Our core is the engine that propels us to full satisfaction, and joy and peace, regardless of what we encounter in life. Our greatest victory comes from understanding where our core is directing us and what drives our core. It is only when we reach our core and begin to learn about ourselves and understand our true value, we find purpose of satisfaction. Being able to recognize our true value provides the motivation needed to ignite the flame of passion. Our core, when align with God as its engine, directs us with great thoughts and influence. Once the core is exposed, we can begin to step out of our history and into our destiny resulting in meaningful purpose and full satisfaction. ***"For, brethren, ye have been called unto liberty; only use not liberty for an occasion to the flesh, but by love serve one another" (Gal. 5:13 KJV).***

Some are able to rise in fortune, fame and wealth; but inner peace is never attained at the end of the day due to unfinished emotions buried within their soul.

Yvonne M. Nelson

Chapter 9

God's Mercies

I spent my life angry at what I expected my childhood to be;. angry at my mother's choice to leave me with her family so they could raise me. Often times I found it difficult to understand where I belonged and attempted to prove my worth or gain acceptance among family or friends. Evaluating my family status and success, I realized that I was not status-quo among them. Instead, I was often reminded of my inadequacy, lack of finances, love of my parents, and the prejudice of their love for me. To sum it up, the feeling of being an outcast was imprinted within my soul. My attempt to find my place within the family led to poor choices which often left me misunderstood, broken, confused and rejected. The disappointments from my love ones, friends and partners led me to a place of emptiness that fostered poor decisions along my life's journey.

As years progressed, I struggled to prove I deserve love and tried to be successful in hopes I could win love from others. This struggle left me broken, empty and feeling desolate as a child and through my adult life. Many years were spent in anger with feelings of rejection that resulted in low self-worth, poor decisions in life and years of bitterness. Webster's Dictionary defines bitterness as an unpleasant sharp taste : feelings of anger; a deep seated ill will$_{(2)}$ **"Let all bitterness, and wrath, and anger, and clamour, and evil speaking be put away from you, with all malice" (Eph. 4:31 KJV).**

That negative energy of bitterness blinded me from recognizing my blessed village of care givers and loved ones, although somewhat peculiar, that surrounded my life. Failure to recognize that, regardless of the mixed emotions I had, I was loved by their full capacity to give of themselves. In honesty they were broken and bruised also in their own ways even though kindness, love and unity was strongly present among us. Moments were spent angry at God and wondering how could He allow such misfortune in my life. Knowing my brothers and not having their love or enjoying any kind of bonding as children growing up hurt deeply within my soul. My parents were off living their own lives forgetting or not thinking of the capacity of my desire for their love.

The perplexity of broken relationships became an emphasis of the negative experiences I had throughout my life, while embracing them deep within my spirit. Nothing positive comes from harboring or focusing on our past, other than allowing the enemy to convince us of our failure and keep us in bondage. Such focus on negative energy only results in missing our blessings and losing ourself, thus delaying our purpose and destiny. *"Cast thy burden upon the Lord, and he shall sustain thee; he shall never suffer the righteous to be moved" (Ps. 55:22).*

We are all engaged in building our consciousness during every waking hour. This work is invisible, silent, and consequently over looked by the bulk of humanity. Nevertheless, it is the most fundamental and far-reaching activity in life. Hour by hour, and moment by moment, we are bringing good or evil, failure or success, happiness or suffering into our lives by the ideas that we harbor, the beliefs that we accept and the scenes and events we rehearse in the hidden studios of the mind. These fateful behavior edifice, upon the construction of which we are perpetually engaged, is nothing less than ourself, our personality, our identity with this earth, and our very life story as a human being.

None of us know how many fine things we have missed through being consumed by our brokenness and painful emotional experiences. No one can be considered really intelligent who does not have a readiness to examine new ideas with an open mind. The answer is that this life we are living today is not the only life and it cannot be understood or judged by itself. Look where you are going, because you will inevitably go where you are looking. Watch what you are thinking and harboring in your mind because it will affect your choices, emotional and spiritual being. Where your attention and focus resides there lies your destiny.

Attention is the key to life as It allow one to focus and be consumed by their interest. Therefore, the consumption of anyone's attention clearly dictates their outcome and purpose, excluding others. God is questioned many times about the lack of awareness one has about their behavior and the effect inflicted on individual emotions and spirit. How can people remain blind to their behavior, selfish attitude and feelings toward others, while continually exploiting them without a stitch of conscious conviction of their actions? Manipulation become a norm and life is all about them that they become clueless of their effect on others. Unfortunately, we will never understand or find the answers to these questions until we recognize the enemy's position in the mist of it all. When we are able to separate the behavior from the individual, we will understand that they too are victims of circumstances. Having recognized this concept, we are able to release ourself from being a victim of circumstance.

The story of the Pharisee Simon came to mind. *Jesus told the story "of a man that loan money to two people of different values that were forgiven and set free of their debts. When Jesus verify from Simon which he believed love the man more after their loan was forgiven. Simon stated he believed the one that owe more. Jesus acknowledge Simon that his answer was correct. Jesus continue to draw reference to the lady with the alabaster box whom loved on him. He continued to tell Simon how he entered his house and no one recognized him, or offered him a glass of water or even washed the dust from his feet. He went on to tell Simon how he had not even greeted him with a kiss or given the courtesy to anoint his head. However, since I have entered the house she has washed my feet with her tears, kissed them and anointed my feet with rare perfume. As a result of her showering me with such love she was forgiven of all her sins" (Luke 7: 40-50 KJV).*

You see, we function under our blinders through life over and over self-centered about what we need or how others should function or behave towards us. We are so focused on self and how people handle or project their actions toward us that we become defensive. Often times we are quick to judge others, criticize their choices or even reject them for the lack of our approval. We also find difficulty in forgiving or being sensitive to others we interact with daily. Never once have we looked through the eyes of others to see their struggles or understand their perspective. Yet we have the audacity to expect God to understand our faults, choices or behaviors through forgiveness. This self-righteous attitude, causes us to constantly miss the blessings that God has provided to us. *"Lead me in thy truth and teach me: for*

thou art the God of my Salvation: on thee do I wait all the day" (Ps. 25:5 KJV).

We spend our lives consumed by our distorted perceptions, chasing material things that society classifies as success, that we miss our destiny and blessings. We want to conquer and solve all our issue as if God no longer has a place in our life. Too busy to pray or just ultimately believe that we hold our destiny in our own hands. As a result, our blinders, governed by our fleshly desires, fight against the process of His will; thus leaving us desolate and unfulfilled within ourselves and our destiny.

His mercies allow us to go through several experiences designed to bring us to the place of releasing ourselves within His presence, trusting Him, and allowing Him to take control of our lives. Truth to ourself and God is a requirement within our inward part, allowing the activation of His healing. Truth that is proven to be sincere, creates honor, moral and ethical values within ourselves and before God. When we are truthful to ourselves we are able to trust God. According to the Bible Jesus is the truth and the way of life; therefore, truth is a necessity to access God into our lives which also activates our faith in Him.

The spirit of rejection resides deeply in the fabric of my soul and mind. The enemy was always there every time I encountered failure, loss of friendship, job or relationship. He wasted no time regurgitating the spirit of rejection in my mind and spirit. The minute something appeared to be a slight obstacle, rejection took control. Through prayer and supplication before God, I experienced deliverance from rejection. There was a week at work I happen to care for separate patients with deceased infants. It just happen to be around the anniversary of my mother's death. For some reason, I spiraled emotionally into a low sad place for days. I also experienced a heavy dull pain over my heart. I began to struggle with the sadness and cried out for God to help me. One night while driving home, I cried out to God and began to worship. I sensed a weight being lifted from my heart and received a vision of a long spiked root attached to the heart. God immediately spoke in my spirit that the root represented rejection from birth. Through being truthful to God and myself, my healing was complete and removed years of bondage. God's mercies once again prevailed in my life. Had it not been for the mercies of God, where would most of us be? His mercies keep us when we could not love or care for ourselves. I know for a fact had it not been for His mercies, I would not be here in a sound mind filled with his love. ***"Remember O Lord, thy tender mercies and thy loving kindnesses; for they have been ever of old" (Ps. 25:6 KJV).***

God provides us every opportunity to pivot through those defining moments within our lives. However, throughout our propelling lifestyle, we are unable to see the markers or even exhale and evaluate what exactly in life we are chasing. Our perplexing life keeps our mind, soul and spirit scattered, so often time we are unable to focus on any one aspect of life or even recognize the blessings we have received. If we would condition ourself to be still, we could connect to our inner emotions and hear the voice of God communicating with us. ***"Therefore we ought to give the more earnest heed to the things which we have heard, lest at any time we should let them slip" (Hebrews 2:1 KJV).***

If we could just pause for a moment and remember the God of the universe that created us for our individual destiny. We would be able to clarify what in life we are chasing and justify these defining moments to seek God's purpose for us. ***"And we know that all things work together for good to them that love God, to them who are the called according to his purpose" (Rom. 8:28 KJV).***

I went through a period in my career where I continued to encounter the same issue of being attacked with lies that cost me my income, contract and integrity. My integrity is all I have and have protected it throughout my life; yet it was always under attack in such a way that I did not even have the opportunity to defend it. The enemy would always and quickly attack my self-esteem, leaving me to feel I was at fault. Family members and friends questioned why I always encountered such attacks as if it was something I instigated. My last attack brought me to a place before God asking Him why He allowed the enemy to constantly attack my integrity and bruise me. I remember His response was to increase my worship to another level. How does worship relate to the enemy consuming me to the very core of my soul, spirit and emotions?

The symbol of the eagle and his performance of capturing his prey came to me immediately. When the eagle capture its prey, he takes it up to the heights of his flight shakes it and drops it. He then soars down, recaptures it, and take it even higher shaking it and dropping it again. He soars again and recaptures his prey and takes it still yet to a higher level shaking it to death. This illustration clearly explains how to conquer our spiritual and earthly battles through worship. When we focus on worship, the enemy cannot enter the battlefield of our minds; nor can he continue to communicate into our spirit. As we are caught up in worship and connected with the Holy Spirit, we open our soul, mind and spirit to the love and mercies of God to flow within us and fill us with His healing balm.

As I continued to heal and moved towards discovering my place and destiny along these trendy waters, I made a decision to visit my cousin in Hong Kong and tour Asia. My purpose was to discover and connect to my roots, reflected from my mother's genealogy of the Chinese culture. The opportunity to spend time with my cousin opened my heart to see my view of being different or unacceptable within the family was distorted by my perceived notion of rejection. How we view ourself can direct our lives in so many negative or positive ways. In my case, embracing negative conclusions propelled me to a journey of failure, low self-esteem and rejection that really robbed me of family connection and love. Now I clearly understand this spiritually and emotionally, thus bringing me to wholeness within myself.

I was able to identify with my grandfather's Chinese culture, learning that he is Cantonese. Understanding the political view, historical wars and exposure to the museum of history clarified the reasons migration occurred. Having been exposed to the culture and finding comfort in their food, family and religious cultural practices, I could see the correlation to my immediate family. I now understand that unity, love and kindness with no boundaries, flows effortless among my family and is the greatest gift given to me. I also realized that there was great similarity in religious practices, food and cultural practices, with slight variation among the three countries of Asia I visited.

Having the privilege to visit and socialize in depth among the Vietnam natives, I was able to learn the beauty of their hearts for life, God and culture. Visiting the museums and learning the history of their trials and tribulations through wars that were inflicted on them for decades, enriched my life both spiritually and emotionally. This culture was attacked and bombarded through several wars they never initiated. Through them, all God's mercies were surely demonstrated in this culture. One thing that was clear throughout their history is, the lack of technology did not allow the enemy to conquer them. The weapons used to fight these wars were love, loyalty, wisdom, skills, unity and the love for their God. Their love was bonded in unity among the Vietnamese and those from the south to help fight the war. Loyalty to each other kept them focused throughout the war. Wisdom brought together their knowledge that allowed them to focus, create the plan, and organize the movements. But the greatest lesson learned was their resiliency, forgiving nature, and love for their God; demonstrated with their worship, acknowledgement and serving attitude to their God in their temples, homes, business, and among families.

I returned home feeling connected to the Asian side of my family's roots, giving me an appreciation for their intricate love, relationship and commitment among them throughout their journeys. I discovered my spiritual wholeness, with clear understanding of who I am as an individual; and that God had a purpose for me in this life. A bubbling joy deep within from the enrichment of spiritual understanding brought me to a deeper relationship with God. I am left with a wider scope of the power of silence before God; which allows me to develop humility in surrendering my life to the will of God.

We cannot change the requirements of God to fit our situation. Our attitudes from our past experiences ruin our present due to the remnants of toxicity in our soul and spirit. We cannot go forward until we figure out our countenance. If God is giving us a new day and a new opportunity to see life, then it is time to surrender our agendas, emotions, struggles, and flesh to Him. This is accomplished by first acknowledging our need for help and allowing His word to enter us, and bring change in our attitude towards Him and our life style. To change one's countenance, attitude and optimism, one needs to desire God's love until it brings a total make-over within us. When we allow God to attach Himself to us, permitting **Him** to shift us to the left or right away from our desires; we are able to enter the gates of our blessings. Only then will we be able to discover His love and mercies that He has in store for us. ***"Make thy face shine upon thy servant; save me for thy mercies' sake" (Ps. 31:16 KJV).***

> *"None of us know how many fine things we have missed through being consumed by our brokenness and painful emotional experiences. No one can be considered really*

intelligent who does not have a readiness to examine new ideas with an open mind. The answer is that this life we are living today is not the only life and it cannot be understood or judged by itself. Look where you are going, because you will inevitably go where you are looking. Watch what you are thinking and harboring in your mind because it will affect your choices, emotional and spiritual being. Where your attention and focus resides there lies your destiny."

Yvonne M. Nelson

Chapter 10

Grace

We often hear the expression, the Grace of God throughout life, which is acceptable as comfort throughout society. Grace is called upon by individuals, when stress, loss of love ones, struggles in life, etc., as a means of finding strength to continue through the process. Many times people would inquire about my well-being and I found myself responding, it's only by the Grace of God I still have my mind. Suddenly I heard myself saying it and began to question myself what is Grace. It was then I realized I found comfort in Grace; but did not understand what it really meant. I began to research the word of God for Grace.

Webster's definition of Grace is a virtue coming from God: a state of sanctification enjoyed through divine assistance.$_{(2)}$ It is reflected throughout the Bible that the transformation of Grace affects our desire, motivation, choices and behavior towards a loving God. Spiritual growth is a slow process through grace as we gain knowledge of God. Paul talks about the grace of God that bring salvation to all. **" *For the grace of***

God that bringeth salvation hath appeared to all men: Teaching us that, denying ungodliness and worldly lusts, we should live soberly, righteously and godly, in the present world" (Ti. 2:11-12 KJV). This grace helps us gain self-control of the worldly and fleshly passions of ungodliness. Grace is the undeserved, unmerited, and unearned favor of kindness from God that is provided to us throughout life. ***For by grace are ye saved through faith; and that not of yourselves: it is the gift of God: Not of works, lest any man should boast" (Eph. 2:8-9 KJV).***

Grace Is the divine ingredient that empowers us to love God. Therefore, when we place our faith in Jesus we have extended grace only through the ability to receive it through faith. Accepting faith allows God into our lives through faith and not of ourselves. It is the compassion and favor of God that draws us to Christ. God desires a relationship with us; and it is through this undeserved, unmerited, unearned favor of God that make that relationship develop. All we need to do is trust and allow God's love to help us keep the law of God. Our actions, good or bad, or our works does not save us or make us God's favorite. *"**But Noah found grace in the eyes of the Lord" (Gen. 6:8 KJV).***

Salvation is only the beginning of eternity, and it is at this level we gain the sight of faith in Jesus. However, many times fear is put in us to live for God or go to hell. So many of us struggle between our humanity, our sinful ways, and our walk with God. We are often characterized by our sins, faith, behaviors and our walk with God. Some feel that they are better than others because they worship differently, dress differently, serve in church and their life style is different from others. If the truth be told, saved or not, most of us are wounded with a sense of shame, condemnation, fear of failure, and a drive for perfection. Yet we believe the lies of the enemy, that we have to serve God out of fear rather than the love of our Father. However, God's unconditional love continues to forgive us each time we fall short of His glory. ***"Therefore if any man be in Christ, he is a new creature: old things are passed away; behold, all things are become new" (2 Cor. 5:17 KJV).***

God demonstrated His grace when He sent His son to die on the cross for our sins. His sacrificial offering of His son provides us with unconditional love that constantly looks beyond our faults and weakness, regardless of how many times we have fallen from His word. Many of us who are convinced we have arrived in God become so judgmental and convicting toward those who are weak within their Christian walk. Our weakness allows God's attentions to be drawn to us. God often uses our weakness to produce strength within our Christian journey from the basic level of our accepting faith to His salvation. ***"But unto every one of us is given*** *grace according to the measure of the gift of Christ"* ***(Eph. 4:7 KJV).***

Regardless of the amount of time we have diverted from His words, God never leaves us nor forsakes us. God's amazing grace provides His love regardless of who we are through eternity. Grace is not the result of our work. Many may believe: their ability to serve God's people, sing in a choir, and all the cultural religious practices in which they participate at church; that they are given more grace than others who are unsaved. Grace is the empowering presence of Christ enabling us to become and do what He desires. The Holy Spirit is our helper that draws us to salvation; and our love for God brings the change of our behaviors and attitude. His word states that love covers a multitude of sins. His sustaining grace is what keeps us. *"…My grace is sufficient for thee: for my strength is made perfect in weakness. Most gladly therefore will I rather glory in my infirmities, that the power of Christ may rest upon me." (2 Cor. 12:9 KJV).*

We have to study the Word with enlightenment from God to become mature in our Christian walk. Developing such a relationship allows us growth in our understanding of Jesus' sacrifice. The greater our knowledge of God's love for us, the greater our appreciation for His love. It is God's grace that sanctifies us and eventually glorifies us into heaven. However, perception is our ultimate reality in this world, even if it is not the ultimate truth. Our reality and perception dictates our actions. Regardless of our impatience, attitudes or our manipulative behaviors, in life our challenges continue to exist among the multitude of choices we encounter along our journey. Grace does not provide us an excuse to live sinfully against the requirement of God's law. Although we are covered by grace, our choices and behaviors have consequences that affect us spiritually and generally in life. *"But grow in the grace and knowledge of our Lord and Savior Jesus Christ. To Him be glory both now and forever! Amen." (2 Pet. 3:18 KJV).*

Seeking to fulfill our own self-righteousness does not remove us from God's grace. Our labor in our process will gain power through the grace of God. When God is perceived as a loving God that sees our faults and loves us unconditionally, we subconsciously become accountable to His law. When we consider the magnitude of His love when He sent His son to be crucified for our sins, we become sensitive and accountable to His expectation of us. As a result, we are able to fall in a loving relationship with Him and with *His* help, change our behavior to be in right-standing with our God. Our weaknesses draws God's attention toward us and He uses them as a testimony. Where sin abounds, grace is much more abounding, thus sin is no match for us. God allows grace to abound above all sins and bondage through Christ Jesus. *"And God is able to make all grace abound toward you; having all sufficiency in all things, may abound to every good work" (2 Cor. 9:8 KJV).*

> *"If the truth be told, saved or not, most of us are wounded with the sense of shame, condemnation, fear of failure, and a drive for perfection. Yet we believe the lies of the enemy, that we have to serve God out of fear rather than the love of our Father." "Therefore if any man be in Christ, he is a new creature: old things are passed away; behold, all things are become new" (2 Cor. 5:17 KJV).*
>
> *Yvonne M. Nelson*

Work in Progress

Philippians chapter 4 in its entirety was given to me in my sleep at the beginning of my journey. Over the years it has been unfolding with clarity and understanding throughout my experiences. In my weakest moment, I dreamt seeing Jesus in the Garden of Gethsemane praying and as I cried out He rose to touch my head saying "Maximized Grace, Maximized Grace is all you need". These two tools has been my source of strength through all my struggles, pain and brokenness. Throughout these years I was stripped to my core, exposed to pain and restored through the Grace of God. Learning to trust God was the first step in my restoration process. Honestly, my pain and brokenness, with God and myself, were the keys to opening my soul. With this transparency, I gave God the permission to invade me, break me, heal me and restore my emotional mindset. This process allowed me to learn to forgive both myself and others who had any influence in my life. Through forgiveness, we are able to free ourselves out of bondage and develop a Christ like heart that functions from His grace. As a result, I am redefining relationships from the family imprint that was filtered down as a fundamental guide.

Understanding that a relationship is reciprocal in any interaction, provides an opportunity to extend ourselves. Being able to extend ourselves, we learn to open our hearts to develop and receive a state of emotional connection with people. This is another facet of Love. The intertwining of love, relationship and trust provided a vision and connection with our emotions. God is love and learning that His love is unconditional without painful or hidden motives, made it easy to trust in Him. As a result of learning to love spiritually, God was able to impregnate my soul, spirit and mind to extend myself to His love, self and others. How amazing is God's love? Just knowing that it is free, without hidden agendas or abuse. All because of His Grace and love I have learned to embrace how valuable I am to Jesus and myself.

The final process is accepting that it is okay to be weak without feeling embarrassed. Our weakness sets off an alarm which attracts God to move and use it for His Glory. The greatest lesson on this journey is being able to trust God, acknowledge and accept my weaknesses and surrender to the love of God. I am still a work in progress as I watch for His greatness within my life. It is with great love I encourage and challenge all my readers to do the same.

Father God we thank you for the completion of this book. Let it not be just a book that fill the shelf but a book that draws readers to the light it represents. I pray that this will be a book manifested to go forth to bring freedom of all those who are expose to the contents. May the words manifest itself within the soul and spirits of each reader to break yolk, generation bondages and bring deliverance of healing and finding you Jehovah the author of and finisher in their lives. God may you take dominion over their life and mindset, break roots and every foundation of all the troubles in their homes, families, business, work places, and destroy all evil activities around them and their children. The voice of the Lord shall defeat all their enemies permanently. May the Grace of God bring salvation, sustain and empower you all. Amen.

I challenge you to rise to the occasion and allow yourself to be healed and find your Shoe (faith) that leads you home to your father and your destiny.

References

Unless otherwise stated all Bible Verses are taken from biblegateway.com/King James Version (KJV), Public Domain in United States

Unless otherwise stated all definitions are taken from the Merriam-Webster Dictionary. Retrieved from https.//www.merriam-webster.com/dictionary

Freire, P. (1994). Pedagogy of Hope. New York, NY: The Continuum Publishing Company.

Greene, M. (1988). The Dialectic of Freedom. New York, NY: Teachers College Press.

CPSIA information can be obtained
at www.ICGtesting.com
Printed in the USA
LVHW032109210322
714006LV00010B/745